Contents

Human

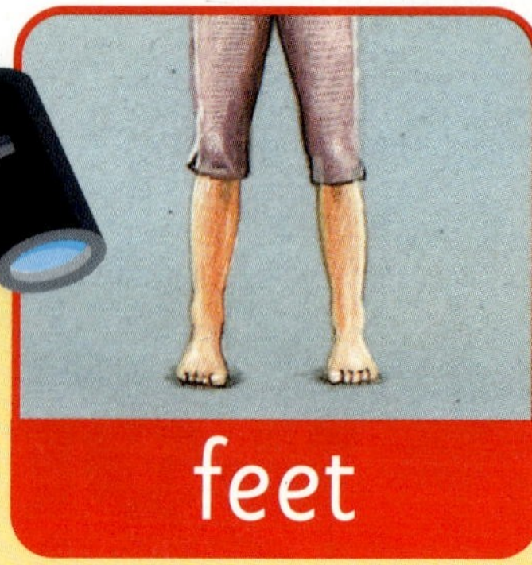

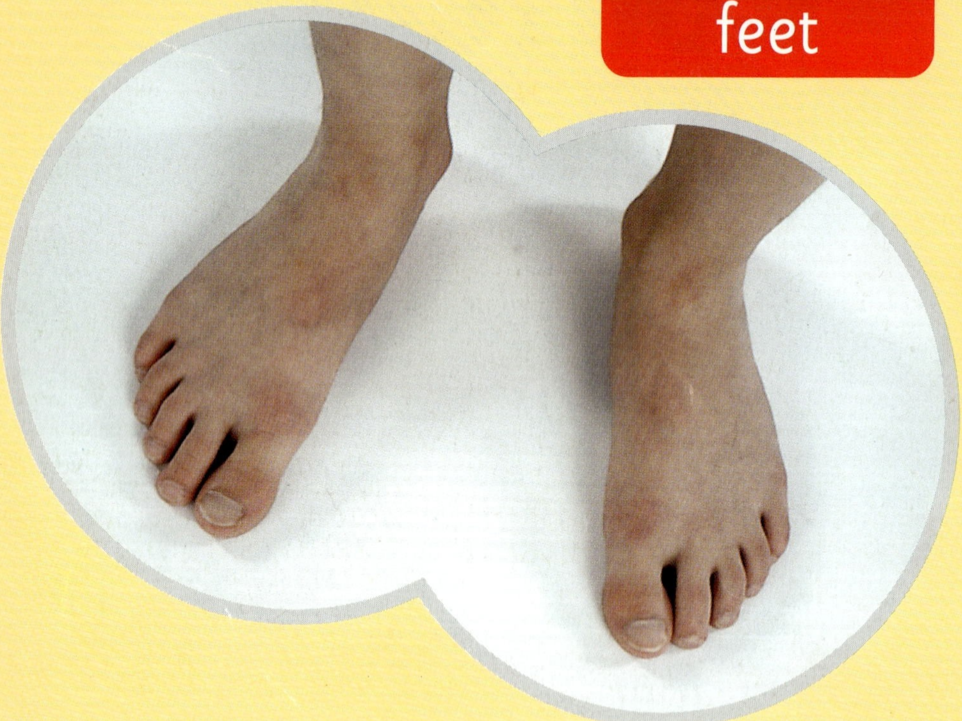

Human feet have five toes.

They help humans to balance.

Swan

The swan has webbed feet.

Webbed feet are good for swimming.

Mole

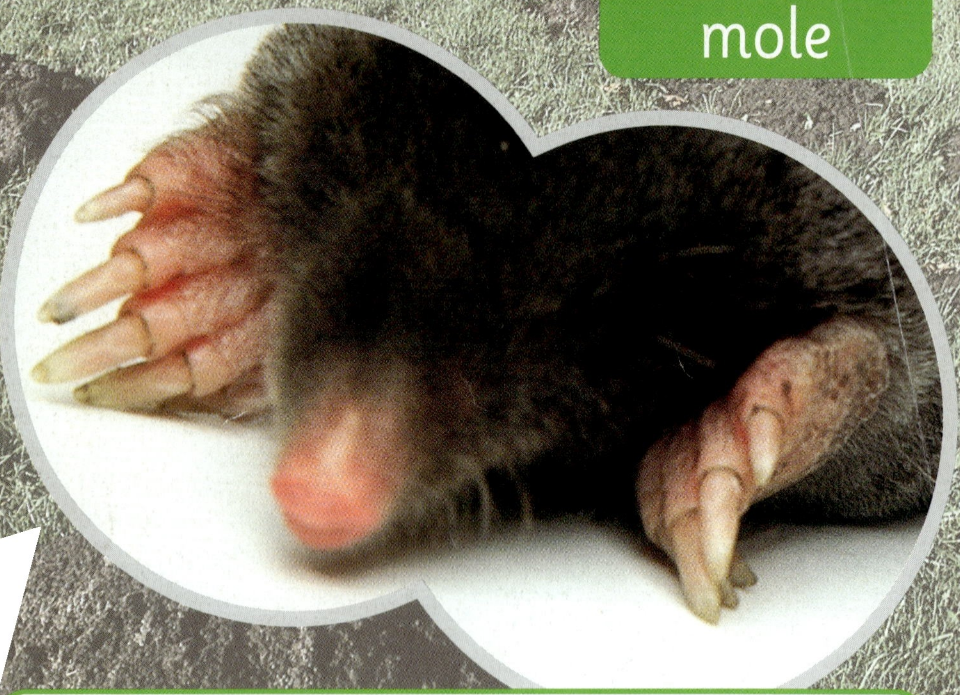

The mole's front feet are like spades.

They help the mole to dig quickly.

Reindeer

Reindeer have feet that spread out.

They help the gecko cling to walls.

Tiger

The tiger has claws on its feet.

They help the tiger catch animals to eat.

Ostrich

The ostrich has very strong feet.

They help the
ostrich to run fast.

Footprints

Animals have different footprints. Can you match each footprint to the right animal?

Index